Revival Poetry and Songs

Kinuthia . f. c

Revival Poetry and Songs

Published by Beaulah Publishers

REVIVAL POETRY AND SONGS

KINUTHIA F.C.

BP

BEAULAH PUBLISHERS

DEDICATION

To all those who cried, "In thy wrath Lord, have mercy," at a time when Kenyans were on the brink of self-destruction in the infamous post-election violence.

I also specially dedicate this book to Apostle Harry Das, the founder of Chrisco Church, who set up a team of intercessors to pray for Kenya after the death of Mzee Jomo Kenyatta(the first President of Kenya). The Lord heard and gave Kenya a smooth transition.

ACKNOWLEDGEMENTS

I thank my dear wife and co-worker in the vineyard, deaconess Joyce for doing the proof-reading and providing invaluable support towards this work.

I'm grateful to my son Chege who provided invaluable technical support all along and my two lovely daughters, Faith and Marrie who really love the things of God, for having faith in me and cheering me on.

Contents

Foreward 1
PROLOGUE 2
Song bird 3
INTERCESSION
The crier 5
OUT OF BLOOD AND ASHES
Fire at the Altar 9
Blood by the hillside 11
Silhouette 14
Stolen vote 17
BETRAYAL
The Covenant 20
Conspiracy of silence 23
I pushed you 26
WILDERNESS EXPERIENCE
The Water is Spent 29
Ziklag Burn! 31
HOPE 33
A day at a time 34
The Dented Skin Drum 36
SORROW
Night Sore 38
Kaa nami 40
Abide with me-Translation of Kaa Nami 41
WORSHIP
Alabaster box 43
Whom do you seek 45
To kneel or not to kneel 46
IN THE POTTER'S HOUSE
The barren rose bush 48
Self raiser 50

Abundance of heart 53
The multicolored coat 55
BLISS
Come ye 58
INTERGRITY
Just the edge 60
Spread your clothes over me 61
Kiuguini kia aria atheru 63
Into the sheepfold -Translation of 'Kiuguini kia aria atheru' 64
The Switch 65
CURTAIN CALL
Days of Elijah 68
Crown 70
ETERNITY
Sipati picha 72
I Can't figure out-Translation of 'Sipati picha' 74
Without end 76
BIBLIOGRAPHY 77

Foreward

"….. a crown of beauty instead of ashes, the oil of gladness instead of mourning and a garment of praise instead of a spirit of despair" Isaiah 61:3

This harvest of poems and songs is best illustrated by the prophetic message by Isaiah. There is a mixture of pain, hope and joy in this work. In several ways, God gives beauty for ashes. In our night, weeping endures. But our morning, which is revival ,is coming.

PROLOGUE

Song bird

The chilly times
Are past
The Elnino
Is over and gone
The fig tree
Has brought forth
Her green figs
The apple tree
With tender fruits
Has a sweet fragrance

The lily fire flowers
Appear on the earth
The time
Of singing of birds has come
I hear a dove
At break of day
Singing from the banana plantation
A song so musical and calm,
So full of hope

Catch us
Catch us
The small weaver birds
That spoil the apples
For our apple trees
Have tender fruits
And the promise
For the harvest is great

Adapted from Song of Solomon part of chapter 2

INTERCESSION

The crier

That's all he did
Weep, weep, weep
Mourn and sob

First time mission
In a far away nation
A golden chance
Trampled upon?

Unsure and in perplexity
Uncertain of what ailed him
In a land far from home
A people needed hope
But..........
Only heartache
Could he pour.

Unease and confusion
Hovered over
The heavily charged
Altar air.
In travail
He wept
They too wept
He knew why.
They didn't.
Though tears flowed

Kneeling on altar
Eyes on heaven

Images flashed
Hippo-like giants
Arose
Baying for blood
Slowly they were rising
In readiness
At opportune moment
Strike!
The peoples of the land
Beyond the rivers of Ethiopia

Suddenly –
The heavens closed
In place came a voice
From some fa-aar place
In finality
Sharp and lucid
The voice said ....

Go sell all
Come back cry
For the people of the land
Lest I judge them

That it was
Neither flesh nor devil
Doubted he not.

Trust and obey.

Taking a big step
He came back saying
Repent! Repent! Repent ....

Up to when?
A case of crocodile
Weeping louder
Than the bereaved.
A prophet of righteousness
Mocked the Bishops
Theirs
Was business as usual-
Gold and silver
Houses and lands
Receive it!
Double, double
They proclaimed

Then in one dusk

Came double trouble
Spears, machetes
Bows and arrows
Fires ,but not of Revival

Blood flowed
In an election gone wild.

The Bishops mused
Maybe ....
Perhaps......
Hushed mournful tones
They exchanged
...Could be
He wasn't a prophet of doom

OUT OF BLOOD AND ASHES

Fire at the Altar

Tell me
I implore you
When they set fire
A very strange fire
On the altar
Where were you

You and I
Sang in the choir
Together we had sang down
Clouds of our Lord's presence
In unity of the spirit
Like David and Jonathan
Our souls were knit
So I thought.

Tell me
I implore you
Did you see?
The ring of warriors
The burning arrow
Right into the heart of the altar
Then a terrifying cry
Of battle and death
In a short while all was quiet
Save for the smoldering fire
And billows of smoke
As flesh in the altar
Turned to ashes.

Don't weep for me brother
You chose your tribesmen
I found favor in God's eye
Weep for yourself
By His mercy
You may be restored

I hear thunder storms
It will rain on the remnants
Stains of bitterness
The rains will wash
On ashes too
Rains will fall.

Grass will grow
Long blades will sprout

Where the ashes be
Blades will whistle in the wind
As they carry
The healing call
Far into the heart of the Nation
And the pent of the Church –
The one called by His name.

August 2008.

Blood by the hillside

Man of God
When the driver screamed
We are under siege!
You heard me shout
Jesus!
For the covering of the blood

With more zeal
You cried out
In tongues indiscernible
You bound and loosed.
I knew we were in tandem,
At least for that moment.

Then hell broke loose
Rocks, stones, Iron,
Hit glass and metal
..........drowned
The cry, shouts, screams
Of the dying.

Kitambulisho mkononi
Identity card in hand

You flashed it
A sigh of relief
Can't blame you.
You made out the goons
They were of your tribe
Not the tribe of Judah.

I grabbed your coat edge
Desperate to live
Forcefully ,violently
You freed self
No association ,connection
No baggage

Those hauled from the bus
Sharp silver swords
In hands of
Blood baying youths,
stabbed, slashed and sliced
Deep groans of death
Electrifying the air
..as blood
Like water
Flowed on the hillside

You missed it.
A bit of Jesus in you
A dying soul

Could have seen.
But don't cry for me
My life was in better hands
He shows mercy
To whom He will
I found favour
In His eyes

Cry for yourself
You may be restored
The blood of the Lamb of God

Speaketh better things
The pool of blood at the hill side
It will cover.

Chrysanthemum and marigold
Will grow
And the aloe vera flowers
With the yellow
Of the sand of the shores
Of lake Naivasha

The bees and mountain birds
Will suck with a song
The winds will carry
To the hearts of the remnants;
A song
Never heard before
In the nation,
And by the Church.

August 2008.

Silhouette

I still call you brother
On account of the blood
That was shed on the cross,
Yes, for you and me.

It is still with restraint
That I do it
For I am at a loss
To understand
The cauldron of bitterness
The rage of anger
The steam of vengeance
That drove you against me
On the day of the clash
That led to the crush
That left many in crutches.
You believed their testimony

That I was a thief ?
Did you..
My brother in Christ
My word you do have

Didn't we fast and pray
For a buyer of my junk-car?
Didn't the Lord hear us?

And speedily provided
A deposit for a first matatu.

The rest brother is known to you.

In good faith
Did I believe;
For my good
An sms you sent
As a friend to a friend
A brother to a brother
....that I should flee
..the clashes that lead to a crush
...that left many in crutches
And our nation in a crunch.

The birds of the air
Sing a different song
They say
..go tell it to other birds
of a breed with severe gullibility

For you scouted and guided
The thief hunters
To my parking bay.

Is it true brother you wept?
Silhouetted against
The inferno of
My 30 years of sweat ?

It was too late to weep.
Like the disciples of Jesus
Who slept
Even when He urged them
...watch and pray

You slept on the evil day
And the great thief struck.

Weep no more brother
For I fell in better hands
Not in my assumed kinsmen's
But of the one who died for me.

...........shh.
Hush brother
The freedom train is coming
I hear hooting round the bend
Far along the lake Victoria

It's sharp and urgent
A cry in the lake shore
A call to freedom from
.hatred
.prejudice
.vengeance
To forgiveness, repentance ,reconciliation

The voice
One of own sons
The doctor turned spiritual healer
Traverses the land

August 2008

Stolen vote

Mombasa hakuna matata
It was well with Mombasa
But this time there is a grave matter
For you mourn on her beach
Where you ought to be laughing

There is no suck pipe
To suck out the poison
The scorpion men
Stung you in revenge
For vote perceived stolen
Hundreds of miles upcountry
Far away
From where they knocked you down

In lapses
You saw then didn't see
You felt then couldn't feel
Deep, deep in you
You knew
They were present
More than beasts in an orgy
Possessing, defiling you

Your body
The Ballot
Place of birth
- a great disconnect-
To you,
Still doesn't add up!

Who will show you
Water, oil and perfume
To wash and wish away
The odor,
The foul smell
Of stolen,
Robbed sanctity
Result of perceived stolen vote.

Hush, sister hush
Mum hush.......
Could there be a sea tide
Far in high seas
Dimly in the horizon
That would float
Ships of hyssop and healing oil
That could come to dock.
And heal our beach.

August 2008.

BETRAYAL

The Covenant

You say there was no covenant
But a statement of convenience
That I imagined it all
You couldn't be more wrong
For all I know a covenant it was.

You came running,
An ostrich on fire,
Couldn't run faster,
Your house was on fire
Torn, ripped, with strife
You sought solace
Desperately so.
A worn out bird
Could perch on any tree.
I am that tree.
And you talk of a covenant?

Yes, it is you say
An agreement it was
'Tween me
And you.
An exchange of vows
In broad daylight
Before the All Seeing One
Fifty, fifty
Give and take
Equal partnership
You insist

But listen.........
There was no covenant
No priest
No blood
No Bible
No soil to lick,
No swearing, by the heavens
And you talk of a covenant!

Yes, you say,
A covenant it was
And still is
You say it was binding
And still is
Till death,
Do us part....

Like Jonathan's and David
It's binding
Like Naomi's and Ruth
It can't be broken
Sly as Gibeonites were
As to trick Joshua to a treaty
To a today M.O.U,
Memorandum of understanding
It was unbreakable

But listen,
This memorandum
Gives me memo phobia.
My heart cries memo murder
I say it is shakable!
You say it is not

I say it is breakable
You say it is not
I say it is *bwogable*
You say it is *unbwogable*
Oorh...............
Could it have been a covenant....?
An everlasting covenant
Despite my denial

Oh, show me how to break it!

March 2005

Conspiracy of silence

He is no longer
The little boy
Of the slopes of Mariira and Nyandarua
Grazing on the slopes of Gacharage
Sipping curd from a *kibuyu*
As the winds from the east refresh him.

Now he takes cocktail
Methanol ,millet and mortuary drugs
All in multi colored bottles.
He has no time for winds
East or west breeze
No longer matter to him
Kaya and marijuana weeds
Give him leisure for pressure
He blinks and reels
Can't stand to occasion
His wife has a rag for a man
Gone, kaput, an effigy
His head and heart throb
She lives with a time bomb

Rabbits and water ducks hunting
Is not a sport anymore
He hunts for money
He can also kill for it
And kill for other things too

He has been very hard and brutish
Very hard

And blood doesn't move him
People talk about him
But only in whispers
They say he demands
From friends and foes
Protection money

In low tones
Behind closed doors
They say he is heartless
A Frankenstein

People need not tell the chief
That's no news to chief or thief
They know more than this.

The day
a head
In bus terminus stood
Wrapped in polythene bag
Other parts scattered
Far and wide
All talked

Chief ,thief
Teacher, leech
Sheep and shopkeeper
Village pastor and priest
Area MP
Area councillor
And the Commandant too
They all talked...............
But,In hushed tones

Behind closed door
He is now wanted;
His energy in the politician's campaign
By businessman to ferry stolen goods
Prostitute and pig farmer for protection
and.. village preacher for his soul;
For all souls to the Almighty God belong

But for now
There is conspiracy of silence.

None dare speak
Of the lost innocence
Of the boy from the hill slopes.
His fate seemingly sealed
...For now

I pushed you

I pushed you
To the witch's hut
You suffered humiliation
Your belly sat on.
The fat filthy witch
Rocking on it
Incantation of the weirdo
Causing a hair rise.

In the change-over time
Your political blood warming up
You sought me in the Temple
Coveting my prayer
As you were a political player

I was scarce
As scarce can be
Slippery
As a wet slope side

Sly
Became my middle name
As with olive oil in hand
Hotly pursued
My new flock
No
My political clients
Who for thirty pieces of silver
Coveted my blessing

You saw holes
In your Covering
Stains on his gown
Deceit on his lips
A big trumpet in his mouth
Announcing harvest time

You sought an alternate.
The omen market
With goods packed
A quick pick
Landed you in her cauldron

Forgive me son.
It's my sin
..I betrayed and abandoned you
When in your hour of need
My pastoral care you sought.

WILDERNESS EXPERIENCE

The Water is Spent

In the middle of the wilderness
Under the scorching heat of the desert
Her feet deep in the oven of the sand
Her lips and skin squeezed of all moisture
The winds strong and fierce
As any wind can be in the desert
Trudged on…………..
The cast out slave maiden.

The sparkless eyes of her dehydrated child
Turned helplessly looking
An urgent appeal on his dry face
Pleading for mercy
Against death sentence in the desert.
For having mocked a child
A child
Whose mother had ordered
Cast out the son and the slave woman!

Again and again
He had cried, “Oh mum ,some water.”
The mother cried back,
“We are in the wilderness,
there is never water in the wilderness.”
Under a shrub
She cast the child
A hasty retreat she made
Lest she see the child die
She lifted her voice and cried.

Her eyes being heavy with tears
She could not see beyond the shrub
Then a voice said,
"Open your eyes!"
It's then she saw a well......

Then she knew
There can be water in the wilderness
But one has to wipe away tears
To see the well
Beyond the shrub of death.

Ziklag Burn!

You may howl
Mourn and sob
Roll in sand and dust
But Ziklag must burn

It is a temporary abode
A stop gap
A refueling point,
Not a destination

The eagles' nest
Where the eagles be
When their wings can flap
Must the nest be destroyed
The eagles into space fly
By pace strong wings grow
Their place towers above
The earth-scratching chicken
The twig-happy horn bill
Where storms be
High above mountain peaks
Their abode be

If it's Ziklag
David needed
Ziklag
God would have secured
Ziklag was but a nest
For a nest the men cried

Crown was David's prize
That in Horeb awaited
Not a desert heath strip
From a Philistine captain

HOPE

A day at a time

There are two golden days
Upon which and about which
I never worry:

Yesterday;
With its frets,pains and aches
Faults, blunders and cares
Is passed…,forever gone!
Yesterday was mine
Now it's God's

Tomorrow;
With its fears, perils and large promises
Is beyond my mastery
It's God's day.

In rosette splendor
Or mask of weeping cloud
It will rise….

Save for the star of hope
Gleaming forever on the brow of tomorrow
Shining with tender promise
Into the heart of today,
I have no say over it.

It's God's day
It will pass through His hands
Before becoming mine.

Enough for each day
Are its own troubles

Therefore,
I think
do
journey
one day at a time…

An adaptation of Bob Burdette's prose.

The Dented Skin Drum

The old soot covered drum
That long in some dark corner lay
The skin wrinkled, its strap twisted
Its edges rough and centre dented
None ever thought
It could ever be of use again.

One day a master took it
With a caressing palm touched the skin
Its twisted strap on shoulder hung
His mind intent on making music
The old cracked drum stick in his hand held,

Then from the old wrinkled drum
Dejected and for long silent
Sprang once more, a joyous sound
Reverberating aspirations, hopes and dreams

Any broken life.
Wrinkled and dented
In some dark corner thrust
Never to arouse interest or passion
Can yet be of some use.

The master's hand
Scarred with old wounds
With a dexterous touch
Can mend a broken life
Yielded to Him wholly.

SORROW

Night Sore

He tossed and sobbed
His sore into the night ran
And ceased not
His soul heavy
Greatly troubled
Very sad

No hug or balm
Caress or cajole
Appointment or ointment
Could assuage

He refused to be comforted

Down the memory lane
Great was the darkness
The more he remembered God
The more he was troubled

He mused upon
Withdrawal
Of His helping hand
Extinction of mercy
End of favors
Failed promise
Failed grace

His spirit overwhelmed
His soul as forgotten
As of one sinking into a pit

Then as one rising from death
Said;
Turn to me again
Cause your face to shine

He declared:
The years of your right hand
Oh, Most High
I will remember
Will remember your works
Talk of your doings
Your wonders of the past
Oh Lord!

Adapted from Psalms 77

Kaa nami

Kaa nami
Ni usiku sana
Usiniache gizani bwana
Msaada wako haukomi
Nilipekee yangu
Kaa nami

Siku zetu
Hazikawi kwisha
Sioni la kunifurahisha
Hakuna ambacho hakikomi
Usiye na mwisho kaa nami

Nina haja nawe kila saa
Sina mwingine wa kunifaa
Mimi nitaongozwa na nani
Ila wewe Bwana
Kaa nami

Siti neno uwapo karibu
Nipato lolote si taabu
Kifo na kaburi haziui
Nitashinda kwako
Kaa nami

Nilalapo nikoune wewe
Gizani mwote nimulikie
Nuru za mbinguni hazikomi
Siku zangu zote
Kaa nami

Abide with me-Translation of Kaa Nami

Abide with me
For the night is far spent
Leave me not in the dark, O Lord
Your help is never lacking
I'm lonely
Abide with me

Our days are short
Am attached to nothing
All has an end
Thee who has no end
Abide with me

I need you every day
None other is suitable
Who will lead me?
Only you Lord
Abide with me

I fear not when you are near
Whatever I go through doesn't worry me
Death and the grave don't kill
I will overcome with thee
Abide with me
In my sleep, let me see you
Be my light in the dark
The light of heaven is everlasting
All my days
Abide with me

Song by Angela Chibalonza Muliri

WORSHIP

Alabaster box

Lady twilight
Tears on your face
Ointment in your hands
What a rash
What a dash

Your hair ruffled
Coupled with a smell
That tons of perfume
Would never wash away
Couldn't you restrain?
The table set
A place of honor
For the clean
At least on the outside
White washed.
How did you get in here?
What unnatural force
Catapulted you
To find yourself
Behind the master's feet?

You, you.........touched him
Your background unwashed
Those salty tears
Washing his clean feet
Your golden, silky hair on him.
The tombs spoke
A prophet?
He would have known....

You broke
The alabaster box.
Precious, precious
Oil oiled his feet

What a waste!
They cried

It is your life
Your everything
Offered at his feet.
He turned
You have seen His face

It's for such as you
From heaven, to the earth
From the earth, to the cross
From the cross, to the grave
From the grave ,to the throne
That He came

Whom do you seek

You have not come to a mountain that can be touched
To a cross of brick and mortar
Incense of billows of smoke
Oil of olive tree
And robe of cotton and silk

But you have come to mount Zion
To the heavenly Jerusalem
To the city of the living God
To thousands of angels
To a joyful assembly
To the church of the first born
To God the judge of all men
To spirits of the righteous men
Men made perfect
To Jesus the mediator
Of the new covenant

To kneel or not to kneel

The chief of the General staff
Had sternly said
The new, young
Commander in chief
Can't and wouldn't kneel !
While soldiers stand

But,
He knelt.

The General, hat off
Bowed his head
To the commander's unspoken order.

The CGS and CJ
The CS and all the Chiefs
And the entire Nation
Should have knelt
Before the Lord of Lords
And the King of Kings
For He makes
And unmakes kings.

IN THE POTTER'S HOUSE

The barren rose bush

In the corner of my garden
A rose bush did I get
For yellow roses to bear
Profusely too

Carefully did, cultivate it:
Well watered and ......
Rich soft soil
And plenty of sunshine.

Yet it bore no roses
It was barren of flowers
Not red, pink or white
None at all.
Why?
I asked the florist
From whom did the bush buy
For blossoms of yellow roses

Remove the rich soil
Never a bit of fertilizer put
Earth in place put
And the bush back severely cut.

The bush blossomed forth
The most gorgeous yellow known
For the eyes to behold
And nostrils to smell.

Then I moralized:

The yellow rose
Like many lives be
Troubles and trials
Does beauty
In the soul bring

In the sandiest of deserts
As in the green houses
Do the finest
Of the flowers blossom
The Lord our God
The chief florist
Designs.

Adapted from prose of Pastor Joyce

Self raiser

In labor pain
A midwife's hand
Comes in handy
To bring to birth
May be-
A potential potentate

In the potter's house
Dexterous hands
Delicately roll lumps
To turn coarse clay
Designer pot

In the farmer's field
To a cow
A heifer is yoked
To train to tread corn
And with plough ,plough fields

It's naturally natural
As in nature
So is the spiritual
By another's hand
The bishop was baptized
Someone else's hands
Ordained him
In another's altar
He said, yes I do

But you……

My brother, my son
In another's hands
You have sworn not to fall
In own hands
Self
You want to raise
You say you are self-made.

But listen, brother to Ahimaz
The man
Who went before his day.

You are raw
This is not your day
You have no message for the king
Do not insist
For yours is another day

Like Ahimaz
You may take a short cut
Or make a kangaroo jump
You may leave a trail of dust

Too thick
For others in the race to dust off

But as you appear
Before your King.
As Ahimaz appeared
Before king David,
Dust from head to feet
Sweat trickling to the feet
Do you hold your head high?

Or will you
Like Ahimaz
Sheepishly bow
Sickly declaring;
I know not what it was.

Abundance of heart

You are rich
You are deep
In mystery shrouded

Shades of attitudes
Medley feelings
Variegated lusts

All in pockets put
Neatly packed
Into deep vents pushed
Tucked and hemmed
Far from any eye.

Your secret content.
Like seeds in good soil
Watered and warmed
Await maturity time
For a surprise to spring

No X-ray
Search light
Scan
Vetting panel
Can ever discern.

The fullness of time
Of slit
Squeeze

Spill
It's a matter of time

Oh, heart
Cry for
A scrape
A wash
A purge

The day
Of fire or flood
Of pleasure or pressure;
Dung or gold.
To the surface
Will glide.

The multicolored coat

You stripped him-
The coat of many colors
Given to him by his father
Provoked you
Moved you to jealousy
For he had said
At his sheaf you would bow

Far in the field
Where sheep do graze
You planned to shed blood
Exchange evil for good
Simply he had brought you good

His blood you knew
Against you could turn
So to the pit you turned
The empty dry pit
For an end his dream to put

You couldn't kill his dream
Potiphar's wife's lusts couldn't
The prison chains couldn't
So Pharaoh made him ruler
For the land of Egypt to rule

When he saw you again
Though you sold him for a gain
His coat soaking in goat blood

Causing your father to pain
For you
He felt pain

Before him you did bow
Right to the earth you bowed
Tears he did hold back
So withdrew he to inner chambers

Loudly he wept for you
He didn't want you grieved
Didn't want you angry with selves.
To him ,
He was sent of God
Life preserve for posterity.

Adapted from Genesis: 35-45

BLISS

Come ye

Come, ye that love the Lord,
And let your joys be known,
Join in a song with sweet accord,
And thus surround the throne.

We're marching to Zion,
Beautiful ,beautiful Zion;
We're marching upward to Zion,
The beautiful city of God.

Let those refuse to sing
Who never knew our God;
But children of the heavenly King
Must speak their joys abroad.

The hill of Zion yields
A thousand sacred sweets,
Before we reach the heavenly fields,
Or walk the golden streets.

Then let our songs abound,
And every tear be dry;
We're marching through Immanuel's ground,
To fairer worlds on high.

Song from the Golden Bells

INTERGRITY

Just the edge

The cave was a proper spot
For nature called
He was hard pressed
And it was no respecter of kings

The ruddy lad
In the hind part of the cave hid

His men in excitement
Quoted scripture:
Behold I will deliver
Thine enemy into thine hand

Quietly
He cut the edge of his robe
Just the edge
Not the back or the shoulder
Just the edge
Not his ear or neck
Just the edge of a robe

A spear through his back
He could have driven
He chose not to
Though he had a reason to.

With his heart smitten he said;
The Lord forbid that I should do such thing.

Adapted from 1: Samuel 24

Spread your clothes over me

His heart was merry
A sumptuous meal
With choice wine drowned
Warmth and bliss
Enveloped him
As by the heap of corn
Lay sprawled his body

He was targeted
A mother- daughter-in law scheme.

Armed with savor of good ointment
Perfumed with frankincense and aloes
Dripping with sweet smelling myrrh;
She had kept a close watch.

At midnight
When little stars twinkle
When the night lark sings
And men in bed turn
His feet were in contact;
The body of a well-oiled woman
At his feet lay
A savor of aloes and myrrh
In the air hang

"Spread your clothes over me"
She said.

And the man with the merry heart
Enveloped in warmth and bliss
Right in the middle of the night
Far from mortal beings
Was tempted

Fear not
I will do all you ask
Indeed you are a virtuous woman
This town knows well

"But……"
With high restrain
Boaz said
Wait till the night is past
At sunrise I will take you to one
Who is more entitled to you

So…
In the broad day light
At the gate
Her fate would be known…

Kiuguini kia aria atheru

Nindoka kiuguini kia aria atheru
Aria mahotaniirwo ni Ngai
Aria matuite matua kurugama
Na kiugo kia ma na kia uthingu

Aya matiui gutiganiria
Manjia rugendo matitiganiria x2
Aya mahuana mwathani wao
Aya matiui kuhotwo ni taki

Mitugo yao nimithuranire
Matiri uru mahana ndutura
Na niogi muno kuri nyamu ya thi
Matingihoteka kana matahwo

Ngoro ciao ciiriragiria o Ngai
Matiri u uiguithanio na mehia x2

Nimi cio ciaragia ciugo theru
Moigaga uria Ngai arenda kugwo
Aya matiri uhinga kana muku
Ngoro ciao itherete ta iria

Meciria mao maiyurite uthingu
Aya niaria mathuritwo kuna x2
Matungatagira na ngoro theru
Matienda kuganwo ni ciiko ciao
Meciragia kugocithia o Ngai
Wendo niguo utuma marugame

Anonymous

Into the sheepfold -Translation of 'Kiuguini kia aria atheru`

I have come to the sheepfold of the righteous
They are those whose battles God has won
Those who have made a decision to stand
With the word of truth and righteousness
These do not know how to give up
On starting a journey they never give up x2

They are like their master
They know no defeat

Their ways are righteous
They have no guile in them,they are like doves
They are wiser than the serpent
They can't be defeated or lured

Their heart's desire is God
They don't compromise with sin x2

Their tongues speak righteousness
They speak that which God wants spoken
These have no hypocrisy or jealous
Their hearts are as pure as snow

Their thoughts are righteous
They are those who are truly elected x2

They serve with sincere hearts
They don't look for fame in their works

The Switch

They rolled back
Red royalty carpet
Behind
Each military stride
Bare surface surfaced

With a brass song
His standard flag
Down down went
Another
Up up rose

In a flash
The sword in a switch
Switched
In electric switch
To a new hand.

In a stride
The guard strode over,
The General crossed over.
A stiff salute
Signaled the change over.

The motorcade and armored car
The Seat
And state house Keys
With a military song
Went to another!

Lost,
I reminisced
The greatest switch ever:
A new guard
A new General
A position in Christ
And the Keys
Of the KINGDOM.

April 2013.

CURTAIN CALL

Days of Elijah

These are the days of Elijah
Declaring the word of the Lord
These are the days of thy servant Moses
Righteousness being restored

These are the days of great trial
Of famine and darkness and sword
I can hear a voice in the desert
Crying,
Prepare ye the way of the Lord!

Behold He comes
Riding on the clouds
Shining like a star
At the trumpet call
Lift your voice
It's year of jubilee
Out of Zion's hill
Salvation come.

And these are the days of Ezekiel
Dry bones becoming as flesh
And these are the days of thy servant David
Rebuilding the temple of praise
And these are the days of the harvest
The fields are white already with the harvest
And these are the labourers in your vine yard
Declaring the word of the Lord

Behold He comes

Riding on the clouds
Shining like a star
At the trumpet call
Lift your voice
It's the year of Jubilee
Out of Zion's hill
Salvation comes

There is no God like Jehovah x 10

Song by Donnie McClurkin

Crown

Crowns and thrones may wane
Kingdoms rise and fall
The church constant remains.

ETERNITY

Sipati picha

Mimi natamani
Mbingu mpya
Na mji mpya
Yerusalemu
Aliouandaa
Mwana kondoo
Kwa kunifahari
Na heshima kubwa

Nitakapomuona
Mwana kondoo
Akija mawinguni
Kunichukua
Na malaika
Wakishangilia
Sipati picha
Itakavyo kua

Mimi natamani
Mbingu mpya
Na mji mpya
Yerusalemu
Aliouandaa
Mwana kondoo
Kwa kunifahari
Na heshima kubwa

Nitakapofika
Kwa Baba yangu
Nitasikia aje

Nikilitazama
Nderemo, Vinungi
Na tarumbeta
Sipati picha

Mimi natamani
Mbingu mpya
Na mji mpya
Yerusalemu
Aliouandaa
Mwana kondoo
Kwa kunifahari
Na heshima kubwa

Atakapo sema
Karibu mwanangu
Taabu za dunia
Hautaziona
Ingia rahani
Kwa njia zozote
Kwa raha zangu
Sipati picha

Mimi natamani
Mbingu mpya
Na mji mpya
Yerusalemu
Aliouandaa
Mwana kondoo
Kwa kunifahari
Na heshima kubwa

Song by Neema Mwaipopo

I Can't figure out-Translation of 'Sipati picha'

I desire
New heaven
A new city
Jerusalem
Prepared
By the Lamb of God
To welcome me
With great honour

When I will see
Son of Adam
Coming in the clouds
To take me
With angels
Rejoicing
Cant figure out
How it will be

I desire
New heaven
A new city
Jerusalem
Prepared
By the Lamb of God
To welcome me
With great honour

When I get there
At my Father's

How will I feel
As I watch
Dance
Timbrel
And trumpet
Can't figure out

I desire
New heaven
A new city
Jerusalem
Prepared
By the Lamb of God
To welcome me
With great honour

When He says
Welcome my son
Earthly sorrows
Never to see again
Enter into my rest
Into my joy
Can't figure out.

I desire
New heaven
A new city
Jerusalem
Prepared
By the Lamb of God
To welcome me
With great honour.

Without end

A flower lasts a season
A tree lasts a life time
The church will last for eternity.

BIBLIOGRAPHY

King James Version Bible
Pastor Joyce's Prose
Bob Burdette's Prose

Songs:
Donnie McClurkin
Golden Bells
Neema Mwaipopo
Angela Chibaloza

Notes

Notes

www.ingramcontent.com/pod-product-compliance
Lightning Source LLC
LaVergne TN
LVHW050330160826
845677LV00014B/3576

* 9 7 8 9 9 6 6 0 9 8 0 2 3 *